Afghan Crochet Patterns for Beginners

25 Crochet Afghan Blanket Patterns With Step-By-Step Instructions & Illustrations For All Crochet Beginners

Nancy Gordon

Table of Contents

Introduction

Are you amazed by beautiful, intricate Afghans, but don't know how to make them on your own? Do you wish to make unique, personalized presents and home decor while relaxing and enjoying quiet time by yourself learning crochet? If so, *Afghan Crochet Patterns For Beginners: 25 Crochet Afghan Blanket Patterns With Step-By-Step Instructions & Illustrations For All Crochet Beginners*!

Did you know that Afghan crochet isn't just yet another creative technique? Did you know that its unique, functional, geometric structure makes it suitable for a variety of items? Did you know that you can make quality, useful, gorgeous blankets, throws, pillowcases, and so much more, by just using simple crochet patterns? That's right!

Learning beginner to intermediate and advanced Afghan stitching is beneficial for you on all levels. Not only is crochet proven to benefit your mood and help you relax, but it shows visible development of creativity and cognitive skills! Afghan patterns shown in this book won't only enable you to make anything that comes to mind, but it will help improve sleep quality, boost your mood, sense of control, help you relax, and find more joy in your everyday life! Plus, the road there couldn't be simpler—you only need a hook, some yarn, and this book!

In Afghan Crochet Patterns For Beginners: 25 Crochet Afghan Blanket Patterns With Step-By-Step Instructions & Illustrations For All Crochet Beginners, you will learn:

How to crochet Afghan beginner patterns.

Are you confused about how to start a row, use the hook, or finish your first piece? This book will give you step-by-step instructions from how to make your first slip knot, to how to twist your hook, where to loop the yarn, how many times to stitch, and even the exact motions needed to make simple, easy, and yet intricate-looking blankets, scarfs, shawls, and throws! These instructions will take away any confusion or anxiety over doing Afghan crochet. More importantly, upon learning beginner stitches, you'll be able to crochet the majority of items you might want, but you'll also know how much and what type of yarn you need, how to take measurements, how to adjust your work to different sizes and styles, and so much more!

How do you go intermediate with Afghan crochet?

Upon mastering beginner afghan crochet patterns, you will start learning more and more complex patterns. That way you'll be able to add decorative edges and intricate curves to your work, giving your afghan more richness, complexity, and dimensions. Of course, all of this will be made simple with step-by-step guidelines for how to make different stitches, shapes, curves, and textures. With this, you'll be able to give your work a personal touch and even begin to develop your own signature style. Aside from knowing how to crochet a basic Afghan blanket or a throw, you'll now know how to polish your work and give it more depth and dimension. But, learning doesn't end there!

How to crochet advanced Afghans and take your skills to the next level.

Once you learn how to crochet intermediate Afghan patterns, you'll start learning how to add a variety of shapes, textures, and colors into your work to make it more refined, interesting, and unique! You won't only crochet geometric shapes. You'll begin learning how to make more complex, ornamental, circular, and even animal-shaped patterns! With these skills, you will be able to make unforgettable, top-quality crochet that surpasses craftwork and transcends into art. With skills such as graph Afghan, you'll truly become a crochet expert! Of course, even the most complex pattern will be broken down and sectioned out for you so that you understand how simple and gratifying the process is if you observe it as a simple series of repetitive movements in a certain matter. I guarantee you'll be surprised how complex-looking works can be done so simply with just a little bit of proper guidance!

But, that's not all! You will also learn about alternative, out-of-the-box Afghan applications. You will learn how to make items that didn't come to mind before so that you can broaden your crochet portfolio and begin making universal works. Still, you must be wondering—is it possible to learn beginner-to-advanced crochet by just reading a book? I say YES! I made it my mission to take you through all of the necessary steps using easy-to-understand terms and descriptions. I guarantee that, even if you haven't as much as saw a proper crochet hook before, you'll find these steps easy enough to apply in real life!

But, this book isn't only about the patterns and stitching. There's so much more that one should know about Afghan crochet to do it properly. You need to learn which size hooks to use with particular yarn types and sizes, and of course, how all that affects the look, thickness, and size of your work. Aside from crocheting, this is one of the aspects of the craft that tends to be more demanding for beginners, but don't worry! I'll show you the logic behind matching hooks and yarn so that you're better able to choose the right combination for your work. Of course, one of the basic skills every real crocheter needs is knowing how much yarn to use for different projects, what type of yarn to use, how to change colors, and so on. You will gain insight into intricacies such as these so that you have full control over your work and its outcome.

So, what are you waiting for? The art of making lustrous throws, blankets, and even rugs, is right around the corner! To start, I'll give you all the essential information about Afghan patterns and crochet, from its background to how to take it from traditional to modern. But, to learn all this, you need to head to Chapter 1 and start learning about Afghan crochet. Good luck!

Chapter 1:

What Are Afghan Patterns?

Have you ever come across the terms "lapghan," "throw," or "afghan"? If you have, you might be confused about what these terms mean in crochet. To ease your concern from the get-go, these terms apply to wonderful, easy-to-make crochet blankets and blanket-like awesomeness that you'll soon learn how to make.

But, is an afghan simply a crochet blanket? It could be, and why not? But, if you take the concept behind afghan stitching and apply it to different ideas, you can learn how to make not only blankets and covers, but also ponchos, sweaters, skirts, curtains, home décor, and so much more! Even better, the geometric nature of the patterns can easily transition from traditional to modern if you go for particular colors, shapes, and materials.

The main reason I love afghan crochet patterns so much is that they give you a type of consistent, fabric-like stitching and the freedom to take the thickness of your result wherever you want. Aside from its beauty, crochet can sometimes be limiting if you're looking to make items that can take wear and tear of daily use. Afghan patterns give you enough flexibility with the density of patterns while remaining colorful and ornamental in structure and texture.

Afghan Pattern Definition

Now that you're starting to learn about afghan patterns, let's define the term "Afghan." "Afghan" is a term commonly used for crocheted and knitted blankets from synthetic or natural fabrics. While there is no set measurement for these items, the afghan blankets also resemble throws. But, there are also a few things that make these stitches unique compared to others. Afghan patterns are hand-stitched, with staple colorful yarn crocheted into predominantly geometric designs. These geometric shapes have a decorative role, but they're also highly convenient for their purpose. They give blankets thickness and consistency while remaining soft and flexible.

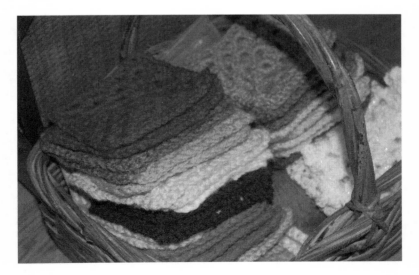

You can use any yarn to make afghan patterns. However, traditional afghan crochet is usually done using camel fibers, angora, and other natural sheep yarn (Casey, 2013).

When it comes to sizing, afghans are usually made to average 5', making them universally suitable for various beds. That way, they can be spread on beds of various dimensions without being too large or too small.

The History of Afghan Crochet

Afghan crochet originated in Afghanistan, as its name suggests. Local people used traditional stitching to make similar-looking, ornamental rugs, while the blankets or spreads the way we know them to date back to the 19th century. They were colorful, and various materials and textures were used to not only make blankets and bedspreads but also rugs. Western civilizations came to know and use the multicolor crochet in the form of shawls and covers at the beginning of the 19th century.

Aside from the color and shape, the distinct geometric look is achieved using specialty afghan hooks. Of course, you can use these hooks for crocheting other patterns aside from afghan. The afghan hook is longer than your average crochet hook, with a cap on its end that lets you add stitches along the way without fearing that the stitches will fall off. An afghan stitch is a square-shaped ornamental delight that can be used to make a multitude of crochet designs from afghan patterns to granny squares.

The term "Afghan" also applies to the southern and eastern Afghanistan Pashtuns. Known for the distinct, colorful karakul wool, colorful rugs, carpets, and other distinct textiles, the region also became known for hand-producing a particular style of crochet that quickly won the affections of early 19th century Americans, who appreciated decorative shawls and blankets that matched the spirit of the time.

But, it wasn't only style and décor that made this stitching so popular. The beginning of the 20th century was the time of poverty, and women across Europe and America found it useful to be able to use leftover yarn and unraveled fibers to create fresh blankets and shawls. The distinct stitching was suitable for repurposing old yarn. It was common for women to save the yarn that was no longer needed, unravel old socks, sweaters, and blankets, and then use this yarn to create fresh, fashionable items. It was also convenient to sew small squares made of leftover yarn together, crafting a patchwork-like lap covering, shawls, or bedspread. Both decorative and functional, this stitching later became known as the "granny square."

One of the reasons why afghan stitching is popular among modern crocheters and knitters is that it helps fix the problem of saturation. Knitting is easy, satisfying, and overall wonderful to do, but you can easily find yourself with extra items that you don't have any particular use for. Furthermore, there's also a great deal of saturation on the market for those who are trying to make a living from their work. While people are quick to share their amazement at your work, there's only a handful of those willing to pay for the amount of work, effort, and creativity that goes into crochet and knitting. For this reason, the flexibility that comes with afghan patterns, and particularly their functionality, is helpful to repurpose some of your old work and yarn. It also lets you think outside the box, and begin making fresh items that will tease the eye of the observer, and find a place in someone's home.

But this universal functionality didn't come out of anywhere. The afghan patterns, also known as Tunisian stitching, combined crochet with knitting in a repetitive way, allowing for many adjustments along the way. Likewise, the repetitive nature of the stitching also made it convenient for beginners to learn it, and even for younger family members to engage in producing functional items for their household. Even children can learn Afghan patterns, which, as you can imagine, was a great advantage for the people who, some centuries ago, had to hand-make the majority of textile items they owned. As the result was quality, intricate, decorative, and useful stitching, this pattern and style were bound to conquer other cultures one way or another.

When looking for inspiration and patterns, you should also keep in mind that some interpretations consider Tunisian crochet to be a distinct form of crochet, while the Afghan stitch is one among the many available under its umbrella.

Another traditional form of western Afghan stitching involved the creation of graph afghans. These afghans were tight and single-colored, with grid-like squares aligned into a perfect grid. Embroidery and cross-stitching were then used to further decorate the design. The more effective use of yarn is another perceived benefit of this style, as Tunisian crochet is said to require less yarn compared to hand-knitting. While Afghan and Tunisian crochet and knitting has a long history, it found a surge of popularity around the 2000s, when the terms began being included in publications.

Modern Use of Afghan Patterns

Nowadays, crocheters are looking for ways to make their work stand out. While preserving the precious traditional and cultural signature marks, the aim is also to pursue modern adjustments that would make the afghans more versatile and suitable to a multitude of styles and tastes. So, what can be done to make your afghan more contemporary-looking? Whether you're looking to expand and develop your craftsmanship, or infuse modern influences into traditional concepts, the following adjustments have been proven to make crochet more appealing to the masses:

- **Simple colors.** Color schemes made out of up to five colors are popular across the board. Whether it's home decor, web design, or fashion, the rule of fives entails determining one bold color to be a focal point, one to serve as a light base, one that either contrasts or complements the former two, and two more "filler" or transition colors from lightest to medium, and from medium to the boldest. A color scheme like this is bound to leave a pleasant impression and is known to be accepted by most people.

- **Simple lines.** Using clean, repetitive, simple lines doesn't only ease the crocheting process. It is also more fashionable and better accepted by both young and more mature people across the western hemisphere. Minimalism and Scandinavian style have a stronghold over early 21st-century esthetics, so hop on the wagon! Minimalist influences entail simplicity, economic use of materials, space, and time, functionality, and utility. Unless they perform a certain role in a design, decorative additions are easily found to be redundant. Whether it's embroidery, stitch, or color, modern esthetics entails making sure that each element has a place in the concept and the big picture of an item, whether it's furniture, a blanket, or a rug.

- **Pastel colors.** Male or female, young or old, very few people resist a well-balanced pastel color palette. If you wish for your Afghan to keep its traditional, colorful appeal but still have a modern touch, you'd be wise to choose a combo of mutually complementing pastels, like white, pale green, mint, and lavender or indigo. Regardless of the lines and shapes you choose, a pastel color theme can be easily incorporated into many personal styles.

- **Monochromatic colors.** Monochrome is another major trend that's here to stay. In interior design, art, and fashion, monochromatic themes are used for an even, eye-pleasing impact with bolder colors. Unlike what you might find in older, more traditional designs, monochrome pallets are based on three to five shades of the same color, from lightest to darkest.

- **Color hierarchy.** Colors of the same "hierarchy" on the color wheel are said to come off as unbalanced and disharmonic, so if you've set your mind on combining greens, blues, and reds, better pay attention to choose complementary shades of each color.

As you can see, there are many ways to make Afghans moderns and fashionable. So, are you up for making some of your own? The next chapter will give you a few more details about how to measure Afghan dimensions, how to determine how much yarn is needed, how to choose the right hooks, and of course, which stitches are best recommended for this type of crochet.

Chapter 2:

Afghan Patterns Must-Know

Top Stitches for Afghans

Even those who are just starting with crochet can easily make full-sized Afghan using the following simple, repetitive stitches (Casey, 2013):

#1 Tunisian Simple Stitch

This stitch is the most beginner-friendly and best known for its simplicity and repetitiveness. Once you get a hold of the stitch, all you need to do is repeat it until you finish your Afghan! For a quick and easy Afghan, it's best recommended to use a thick yarn with a 6mm crochet hook.

Requirements:

- **Yarn:** Size four.
- **Hook**: 6 mm.

Instructions:

Here are the instructions for this stitch:

1. Chain a desired number of stitches for your base.

2. Insert the hook into the second stitch from your hook as you begin your first row forward, yarn over, and pull up, leaving the stitch on the hook.

3. Repeat throughout the entire row.

4. For the second or the returning row, yarn over, pull up, and then yarn over, and pull through two loops.

5. This will reduce your number of stitches, and all you need to do is proceed this way until you finish the returning row.

6. That's it! All you need to do is repeat until you have enough rows!

#2: The Grit Stitch

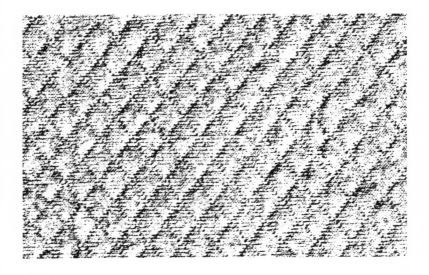

Requirements:

- **Yarn:** Size four.
- **Hook:** 6 mm.

Instructions:

1. This stitch is friendly to all types of yarn and their matching hook sizes. All you need to do is make a chain base, then insert the hook into the third chain from it, and do two single crochets.

2. Next, you need to skip one chain and repeat the stitch into the one after it.

3. Repeat until the end of the row, turn the work, chain one, and skip one to do two double crochets into the third stitch from the beginning.

4. Again, skip one stitch and crochet into the one after it.

5. Proceed with the instructions for the second row until you finish your Afghan!

#3: The Moss Stitch

Requirements:

- **Yarn:** Size four.
- **Hook:** 6 mm.

Instructions:

1. This elegant-looking stitch doesn't require you to count as you crochet, and it lets you just relax and enjoy your work.

2. How to make the moss stitch? Simply chain the desired-size base, making an even number of stitches for the base as you do for the foundation.

3. For the first row, add a single crochet into the second chain from the hook.

4. Chain one, skip one chain, and add a single crochet into the next chain.

5. Chain one and proceed until the end of the row!

6. For the second row, chain one and do a single crochet into the first chain.

7. Skip one chain, chain one, and do a single crochet into the next chain. That's it!

#4: The Lemon Peel Stitch

Requirements:

- **Yarn:** Size four.
- **Hook**: 6 mm.

Instructions:

1. Aside from being quick and easy, this stitch creates sturdy fabrics, which makes it great for more than Afghans.

2. You'll notice that the thick fabrics you make with this stitch make for great rugs and washcloths as well!

3. To make an Afghan with the lemon peel stitch, you first need to create a chain and start the first row by doing a single crochet into the second chain.

4. Do a double crochet into the next chain and then the single into the chain after that.

That's it! All you need to do to finish your Afghan is to proceed alternating between single and double crochets. Make sure to start each row with a single crochet!

#5: The Overlapping Post Stitch

Requirements:

- **Yarn:** Size four.
- **Hook:** 6 mm.

Instructions:

1. This nice-looking stitch is great for soft, chunky blankets.

2. All you need to do is start your base chain and then do a double crochet into the fourth chain from your hook.

3. Next, proceed doing double crochets into each stitch until you reach the end of the row!

4. To start the second row, chain one, skip one, and proceed with doing single crochets into each stitch until you reach the end.

5. For the third row, chain three, yarn over twice, and go down the double crochet beneath the first single crochet, pull up a loop, yarn over, and pull through two twice, which is known as a front post double crochet.

6. Do a double crochet into each single crochet stitch.

7. Alternate between the two until the end of the row.

8. For the fourth row, repeat the pattern for the second row, and again for the fifth row repeat the pattern from row three.

9. Proceed until you finish your blanket!

Afghan Dimensions, Base Chains, and Measurements

Now that you know how to crochet the most popular afghan stitches, you're likely planning to start making Afghans by yourself. While it's great to be able to crochet a blanket, a bed cover, or a rug quickly and easily, the issue of how much yarn to use and how many stitches to account for quickly becomes a puzzle. Now, it's time to learn how to measure your Afghan, supply enough yarn, and find out how many stitches to crochet for just the right size.

In general, despite any instructions that you might find, each yarn is unique, and so is your taste. Aside from the stitch itself, the dimensions of an Afghan, its thickness, and texture also depend on the tension you use. Once you start crocheting, you might discover that you prefer thicker work, which entails adding more tension to your crochet. This will then increase the number of stitches needed for the desired size, requiring more yarn. On the other hand, if you wish for a looser Afghan, you might need to reduce the number of stitches so that your work doesn't end up being too large. Finally, all of this affects how much time it will take you to finish your Afghan, which is important if you're budgeting your time or trying to work crochet into your busy schedule.

With this in mind, it's time to start learning how to properly measure and size your Afghan. Afghans, while being super easy to make, are extremely difficult to alter. Choosing that ideal number of stitches and the right tensions becomes that more important. To start, rely on your measuring tape to decide how many stitches each of your rows will have. If you want to make universally fitting sizes for different beds and surfaces, you can rely on three common measurements (Goldberg, 1987):

- Afghan, which, in its full size, measures 50x65".
- Lap blanket, which measures 35x40", and
- Baby blanket, which measures 25x30".

However, not all Afghans have to be the same. You might find a baby blanket motif you like and wish to use it to make an Afghan, or vice versa. So, what should you do then? The easiest way is to use a measuring tape and calculate how many stitches in height and width make for an inch, and simply re-do your calculations. Aside from this, the amount of yarn and the number of stitches that you'll need also depend on your motifs:

Simple stitching is easiest to measure and size. All you need to do is make a swatch and count chains and stitches that went into the work, which will give you the exact number of stitches needed for your desired size. To determine the right amount of yarn, you can, again, calculate how many times your desired size is bigger or smaller compared to the sample size, and get the right amount of yarn.

Consistent motifs are a bit more complex to measure and calculate. Swatches are the best here as well since the amount of yarn and the number of stitches doesn't directly affect the size of the Afghan. Instead, a portion of the work goes into creating its texture. If you encounter a motif that's too difficult to measure and count, you can try and count the motifs instead. You can count how many stitches go into a single motif, how many motifs go into a row or an inch, or you can simply grab a measuring tape and calculate how many inches a pattern measures, and how that fits into your selected size.

Inconsistent motifs. If your patterns aren't fully consistent across the Afghan, there are several ways to make modifications. You can either decrease the number of single and double crochets between the motifs to increase the size of the Afghan, add rows of simple stitches, or do test swatches to see how different stitches and patterns affect the Afghan dimensions. You can also add several simple-stitched rows around the edges of the work or increase the visual size using tassels. All this depends on your level of experience with crochet and how you want the work to turn out.

In any case, modifying Afghans, while difficult, is great because you're adding your unique touch to the work. If you're a beginner, I advise making swatches or pattern samples for five to ten inches before starting your work. If the chosen motif is inconsistent, do a swatch for each distinct motif. This way you'll get plenty of practice before you begin working on your final sample and you'll get a better hold of counting and measuring!

Alternatively, you can change the size of the yarn to either decrease or increase the size of the work. Not only the weight but also the design and consistency of the yarn will affect the size of the work. You can rely on mathematics to a certain degree for this—the percentage in which a chosen yarn is heavier or lighter, compared to the sample yarn, will affect the size accordingly. But, this doesn't always have to apply. You may have to use more or less tension on the yarn for the same pattern result, which also factors in the calculation. For this reason, it's best to decide what to do based on swatches. Do a sample swatch with your selected yarn and simply measure how bigger or smaller it is compared to the sample. Optionally, you can consult staff in the store you buy yarn in or the manufacturer directly for advice. It might sound exaggerated to go through all this effort, but if you're investing time in making an important piece, or spending money on top-quality yarn, ending up with an item that's the wrong size is just a shame. Now that you know how to properly measure your work, let's answer one more daunting question: How much yarn do you need for your work?

Which Yarn to Choose and a Hook to Match

If you're just starting with Afghans, the issue of the right amount of yarn to get suddenly becomes that more important. Afghans are valuable items, and the last thing you need is to run out of yarn halfway through a project. Even worse, you might be unable to get more of the same yarn that you used for the project, which could potentially ruin your idea! Moreover, choosing the wrong type of yarn for a particular pattern or motif could take away from its beauty, texture, and even compromise the size you're aiming for. So, how do you choose yarn? You can rely on the following suggestions:

Keep it simple. In the variety of yarn types, I suggest reducing your choices to wool, acrylic, and cotton. Learning about the qualities of each type will take time, but by the end of it, you will develop your own taste and preferences. Each person crochets in their unique way, so you'll find that you're more comfortable using some yarns than others. Moreover, different types of yarns have their own best use. Wool is best for thick, cozy blankets and Afghans, while cotton is naturally cooler and will produce lighter, more breathable fabrics. Acrylic is more versatile in style and color and could be a great choice if you're more focused on the appearance and design than the functionality of your items.

Wool yarn is a great beginner option since wool doesn't show tiny mistakes and imperfections as much. Depending on the stitching you choose, those little mistakes could add to the uniqueness of your work. But, wool may cause allergies, irritations and is naturally a very sensitive material. You can get wool yarn that's machine washable and even tolerates high temperatures, but these yarns will be more expensive.

Cotton, on the other hand, is lighter, cooler, and thicker. It will be a great choice if you want to make an Afghan for spring and summer or a universal piece you can either throw over your bed or use as a shawl. The downside, of course, is that it won't keep you as warm as wool and it's not as elastic. Working with cotton as a beginner will take a lot of practice when it comes to tension since any variations will affect the evenness of your patterns. For example, if you crochet tighter on one side of the row than the other, your patterns will be smaller, and the overall size of the row will reduce. But, if this happens with wool, you can simply stretch out the work and forget about it.

The acrylic yarn is highly versatile in color and texture but tends to split apart as you crochet. On the other hand, acrylics are more affordable, which makes them great for practice. If you're a beginner and you're learning new stitches, the acrylics will be a great option for making numerous swatches for future reference at a very low cost. Acrylics are great for intermediate and advanced crocheters as well. If you're planning to make a more complex design and you wish to try it out first on a cheaper material, what better choice is there than acrylics!

But, how do you decide on the right yarn weight? Typically, yarn is categorized by numbers one through seven (Goldberg, 1987). The larger number indicates the greater thickness. Beginners are recommended to work with yarns labeled with numbers three and four, since these sizes are easiest to master, and they're easily used for most projects. Of course, you're entitled to your own taste and preference. If you wish to work with a thinner or chunkier yarn, you can always slow down the pace and take extra time to learn how to work with it.

When it comes to pairing the yarn with hooks, the label on the yarn will tell you the exact type and size of the hook to use. When it comes to yarn texture, beginners are advised to start with a smoother yarn. You will have better control over it and it will be easier to locate the right stitches and chains when crocheting. But, again, chunky yarns do come in some of the most amazing designs and crochet isn't rocket science. If you're infatuated with a particular yarn, go for it, and simply give yourself extra time to work it out. It is also said that dark colors are typically easier to work with than light ones because they show stitches and gaps better. But, if you like bright-colored yarn, you can always pause, lightly stretch the work between your fingers, and find the right gap to insert your hook.

When it comes to yarn price, you will find plenty of variety. As in any hobby or industry, a handful of brands stand out as most popular or luxury, but you don't have to splurge on yarn to get a quality result. Research and read online reviews, particularly those that compare more expensive against more affordable brands. Furthermore, when choosing which yarn to buy, make sure to compare the yardage on the labels. The difference in prices doesn't always reflect quality—it may be about the amount as well. When making a price comparison, make sure to compare the yardage as well. Color is another important consideration when it comes to yarn selection. When working on a larger piece or a set of different pieces, color consistency is extremely important. The best way to get that is to make sure that color information on one label, or the 'color lot' fully matches the one on the other. Finally, there's plenty of choice for anyone who doesn't wish to use natural wool. You can also get vegan yarn if you don't want your material to come from animals, and likewise, you can get organic yarn if you particularly care about the origin and quality of your work.

Now that you know how to choose the right yarn, let's talk a little bit more about the choice of hooks. Of course, you're best off choosing a hook that's suggested on the label of your yarn, but it's also great to know some Afghan crochet hook trivia just in case. Particularly, if you're working with Tunisian stitches where the loops will remain on the hook, you need to have the right selection by your side.

Tunisian crochet hooks are designed to easily crochet both forward rows, where you keep the loops on the needle, and the backward rows, where you gradually pull the loops. Tunisian crochet hooks are unique for the stoppers on their ends, which help keep the loops on the needle and prevent them from falling off.

When choosing an Afghan hook, you should take its material into account. Afghan or Tunisian crochet hooks can be made from plastic, aluminum, bamboo, or wood. While the size of the hook and its shape play the most important role in how your work will turn out, different materials have a different feel and weight in your hands. They also have different levels of elasticity, which is all relevant if you're planning on committing to doing daily crochet, and particularly if you plan on taking your hobby to the next level and dive into being a professional.

When it comes to the length of Tunisian hooks, they're most relevant for doing larger projects. Regular hooks will work just fine for throws and baby blankets, but full-size Afghans might use larger hooks that can support your work. This particularly goes if you're working with different Tunisian stitches, where the loops need to remain on the hook. For standard Afghans, hooks measure anywhere between 10 and 14 inches in length. When choosing a hook, keep in mind that you're always better off with the lengthiest hook you can handle. Crochet is best done when your loops are loosely and evenly spread across the hook so that you can see and count them all. So much talk about Tunisian stitches, right? But, aren't they supposed to be the simplest? It's true, but the simplicity of the stitch here comes with the necessity to pay extra attention to your loops, make sure not to pull through too many, and of course, have a clear, spacious layout for tackling several balls of yarn at once. Let's say that you have over 30 or 40 loops on a short needle, plus several chunky wool threads that you need to keep track of which to weave and which to work with. Given the creative freedom with Tunisian stitches, you may even choose to have two yarns to work with and another two to alter. Imagine all those loops in different colors squished together on a tiny hook! How are you even supposed to keep track of your work? The answer is—by choosing the hook of adequate size and shape. This is where the shape of the hook comes into play, and you can choose between:

Straight. Resembling knitting needles, these hooks come in different lengths and sizes. The larger the hook, the larger your work. Your straight Tunisian hook will have a stopper at the end to hold your numerous loops. These hooks are great for larger projects done with Tunisian stitches but can become too heavy and hard to handle if you're making large Afghans with complex motifs. Imagine having to work dozens of Tunisian stitches and then moving to make ornamental squares with a giant hook in your hands. Doesn't work well, does it? In this case, you can either alter hooks or if you want to use the same hook all the way through, choose a corded needle.

Corded. As the name suggests, this needle is made from a cord past the first six inches. With a corded hook, your large, chunky, heavy fabric will fall nicely and comfortably into your lap, with stitches and loops still nicely contained and visible. The downside to this hook, of course, is that you don't have a clear overview of the work in your hands, but it may be the best solution for certain projects.

Interchangeable. Once you advance your skills, you can also get sets of interchangeable hooks that allow you to mix and match hook, cord, and stopper sizes. That way you can assemble a tool that works specifically for your project and personal taste. Once you're done with the project, you can then take the Franken-hook apart, and use a completely different combination of its parts for your next Afghan. Versatility is the major upside of this option, while the downside is that you need to have a thorough knowledge of which parts go best with your selected yarns for the hook to work for you. If you're a beginner, you might not be fully familiar with which stopper sizes and cord lengths are best suited for your project, which can unnecessarily complicate your work.

Ultimately, you can simply determine the size of your Tunisian hook by looking at the yarn label, checking the recommended hook size, and then going two sizes up for your Tunisian version. This is because Tunisian stitches are typically more condensed and working them using standard needles may result in curled or insufficiently elastic fabric. If you go a couple of sizes up, there's less risk that your work will curl or come out too thick. If you're looking for the right chord, a small recommendation is to base its length on the lengthiest row of your pattern, just to make sure that it can hold your work all the way through.

Chapter 3:

15 Beginner Afghan Patterns

Pattern #1:

Bulky Yarn, Easy Blanket

This pattern is an easy first-time Afghan project for anyone who has just begun learning about crochet overall or had just started making Afghans. The upside of this pattern is that it produces a decent-sized blanket using soft, bulky yarn, while not a lot of time is required to do it.

Requirements:

- **Yarn:** Size five chunky yarn
- **Hook:** 6.5-9mm

Instructions:

Here's how to crochet this pattern:

1. Start by making a slip-knot. To make a slipknot:

    a. Loop a strand of yarn over and pull a piece of yarn through the loop. Use a 9mm hook.

    b. Pull the hook through the loop, huck the yarn and pull through the loop.

2. Going forward, I'll use the expression 'yarn over', which here means to pull the yarn through a loop, twist the needle over it to pick up the yarn again, and pull it through the loop.

3. Repeating the said motion creates a chain that looks like a braid.

4. Now, it's time to pull the hook through the first 'bump' in the chain after the one on your hook.

5. The motion is the same—yarn over along the chain, then pull through each of the bumps along the way.

6. Don't be afraid to slow down! This motion seems complicated at first, but it will soon become automatic and you'll be able to do it without thinking.

7. Do a 'single crochet' ("yarn over and pull the yarn through") the entire chain until you reach the strand where you created the slipknot.

8. When you look at your work, you will now see two braid-like chains that look attached. You can, by all means, make a blanket or a scarf simply by repeating the single-crochet chains until you achieve the desired length and width. But, here you're learning how to make Afghan patterns, so we'll now begin creating geometric shapes from the yarn.

9. The two-chains you just created will serve as a frame for your blanket. Once you're done crocheting the second chain, do a chain-three crochet upwards from the edge of the frame.

10. A chain-three means to yarn over and pull through three times. This will be a beginning of a rectangle-shaped pattern that you'll be making.

11. Proceed by yarning over and pulling the hook through the next "bump" or loop, only this time

do a double crochet. This means to yarn over and pull through twice.

12. You'll now have three loops on your hook. Pull the yarn through its closest loop, and repeat once more.

13. You'll now have a single loop on your hook again.

14. Proceed by doing the double crochet, as in the previous step.

15. Once you reach the end, insert the hook into the bottom loop (the same row in which you began crocheting on the opposite side), yarn over, pull through, and then proceed to chain three in the same pattern as in steps 5-7.

16. Repeat for as many rows as you wish.

17. Once you're finished with the last row of your double crochet by repeating steps 5-7, you can simply tie a knot after the final stitch, and you're done!

Regardless of the size you choose, your blanket will be warm, and think, if you use soft, bulky yarn, it will feel tender and soft. Are you ready to learn your second Afghan pattern?

Pattern #2:

Triple Yarn Single Crochet

For this project, you will need a size 4 worst weight yarn of over 3000 yards. Unlike the previous, this blanket is done using the triple yarn, or crocheting using three strands at the same time using a 15mm hook.

Requirements:

- **Yarn**: Size four worst weight, 3000 yards for the whole Afghan.
- **Hook**: 15mm.

Instructions:

1. Hold three strands together.

2. This is done easily by using a single yarn from three different balls of yarn.

3. They can be the same type, size, and color, but you can also mix different types of yarn for a more textured, colorful blanket.

4. Make a slipknot and chain 50-100, depending on how large you want your blanket to be. As in the previous pattern, you'll get a braid-like chain.

5. Once you're finished with the chain, begin with single crochets along the length of the chain.

6. You'll have two loops on your hook after each new stitch, so yarn over and pull through the two loops until you have a single loop.

7. Once you reach the last loop of the chain, pull through and do a single crochet.

8. Turn the work over and go through the front loops, doing single crochets in the opposite direction.

9. Repeat steps 3-4 across the desired size of the blanket.

10. Once you are finished making your Afghan, you can either single-crochet along the edges of the blanket, or you can make tassels.

11. If you want to make the tassels, the process is simple.

12. You only need to take three strands of the desired length and fold them in half to make a loop. Bring the loop to one of the edge loops, pull the hook through it, yarn over the tassel loop, and pull through.

13. Then, yarn over the outer edge of the blanket, pick up the tassels with your hook and pull the entire length of the strands through.

Pattern #3:

A Simple, Two-Colored Baby Blanket

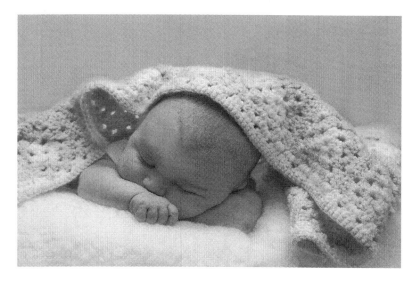

For your third project, you will make a two-colored baby blanket. You can use either two different yarn colors, or you can get specialty baby-blanket yarn that's suited for gentle baby skin and conveniently features soft, baby colors. Typically, you'll need around 20 yards of 300g wool, but this can vary depending on the material. Remember, you have full control over the size of your work. If you're not entirely sure if the yarn will suffice, you can always get extra. You can also use a measuring tape to determine the desired size of the blanket.

Requirements:

- **Yarn:** Size three to four, approx. 20 yards.
- **Hook**: 6-8mm

Instructions:

Here are the steps for this pattern:

1. Start with a slipknot and make the foundation chain. For a baby blanket, you will need around 50 chains.

2. The exact number will depend on the yarn, so rely on your measuring tape.

3. Once you've finished your base chain, do a half-crochet. Insert the hook in the loop next to your first loop, yarn over, and pull through.

4. Proceed to yarn over and pulling through all three loops until you have a single loop.

5. Repeat the step for the next chain on your base row and proceed until the end.

6. Chain two, turn the yarn over, and repeat the rows as many times as you wish or until you complete the desired size.

7. For this blanket, do a double crochet each time you complete a row.

8. Keep in mind that, considering that you're pulling through three loops at once as you crochet, you will have three yarn threads above

the chain gap where you're supposed to insert the hook.

How to change yarn colors? Once you finish a row with a single color, cut the thread and tie in a thread from a different color. Proceed with crocheting by repeating the steps.

Pattern #4:

The Fishbone Half-Stitch

Requirements:

- **Yarn:** Size four.
- **Hook**: an L9 or a 5.5 mm.

Instructions:

1. Start a slipknot and chain for anywhere from 50 to 100 chains.

2. Yarn over and insert the hook into the third stitch.

3. Yarn over, pull through, and pull through the two remaining loops.

4. Proceed until the end of the first row, chain one stitch, turn the yarn over, and proceed crocheting as many rows as you wish.

5. In this pattern, every two rows will create a fish-bone-looking pattern.

6. Making repetitive moves, turning the yarn over, and working in different directions will produce this distinct pattern.

7. Keep in mind that this pattern also has a right and a wrong side.

8. The side that faces you while crocheting is the right side of the work, while the side that faces outwards is the wrong side.

9. You can change colors as you wish, by pulling a new color in at the end of the previous row, and clipping and weaving in the previous.

I like this pattern for shawls, blankets, and ponchos alike. The upside to this particular stitch is that it's very thick and functional. It will keep you warm and, if you choose extra soft wool, you'll love having it by your side every single day!

Pattern #5:

The Simple Brick Pattern

For this pattern, you will need a ball of chunky yarn.

Requirements:

- **Yarn:** Size five.
- **Hook:** 6-12 mm.

Instructions:

1. Start with a slipknot and pull a 9mm hook through it.

2. Your chain should be consistent, but not overly tight since you want a soft, loose blanket.

3. Start chaining around 80 chains.

4. If you prefer, you can determine a desired size for the blanked and then use a measuring tape to determine the right length of the chin.

5. Once you're done with the base chain, crochet another row with a single crochet.

6. Begin the next row with a chain two, which you'll count as a double crochet.

7. Proceed to do double crochets along the chain by yarning over and pulling through each following base chain.

8. After pulling through the first time, yarn over, and pull the hook through two loops, repeat one more time, and then use the one remaining loop to crochet into the next chain.

9. The goal for the next row is to repeat the steps from the previous row, but this time, place the chains between the chains from the previous row.

10. Once you've finished your first row, you'll notice a rectangle-like structure in which there's a space between two chains.

11. In previous patterns, you'd proceed by crocheting into the chain above a chain from the previous row, making it look like the rectangles are sitting one on top of the other. Here, you

want the top rectangles to "sit" on top of the gaps between bottom chains, creating a brick-wall-like pattern.

12. To achieve this, you will proceed by doing the previous step, but, you will insert the hook into the gap between the chains.

13. Remember, once you reach the end of each row, work in the last stitch, and start with a chain two and dip the work.

14. If you want to change colors, the best way to do it is to snip your previous yarn at the end of a row, leaving a couple of inches to weave it in.

15. You will still have the loop from the previous yarn, and you can simply yarn the new thread over and pull through.

16. The new color will start with the new row as you start the double crochet.

17. The spot where you added the second yarn will now have two different threads peaking out.

18. There are several ways to remove the hanging threads.

19. The easiest is to tie these threads into a tighter knot that doesn't show through the work and simply snip off the excess.

20. The second way, more preferred by professionals, is to weave them into the work with a needle. You can do this by pulling the thread through a loop in your needle, and then

weaving it into the threads along the edges of the work.

21. The key here is to weave through threads, and not in the spaces between them. Also, to further secure the weave, you should go back and weave the thread through the previous weave-in.

22. Of course, weave the threads into the row of its color for a cleaner look.

23. Now, it's time to learn how to crochet along the edges of the work so that it's more secure and clean-looking.

24. Once you reach the end of your final row, do single crochets along the edge.

25. Instead of tying a knot and snipping the excess thread, do a single crochet on the final remaining loop, and then rotate the work 90 degrees and begin inserting the hook into the chain of the row, and not the gap beneath it.

26. Yarn over, pull through twice to have a single loop on your hook and proceed by going into the chain above the next gap.

27. Repeat this step along the edges of the entire blanket.

This throw is beautiful and decorative, but keep in mind that it won't be very thick or warm.

Pattern #6:

A Basic Cross-Stitch Afghan

Requirements:

- Yarn: size five, chunky
- Hook: 11.5mm

Instructions:

1. Make your slipknot and chain a desired-length chain.

2. Do a half-double crochet into the third chain from the beginning of the second row, and

proceed with a half-double crochet along the length of the row.

3. Make a chain-two and a half-double crochet.

4. Now, you will use a pattern called half double crochet cross-stitch.

5. How do I do a half double crochet cross-stitch? Skip one stitch from the previous one, and do a half-double crochet.

6. Next, yarn over and pull through the stitch that you skipped.

7. Stretch that stitch, yarn over, and pull through all of the loops on the hook.

8. You'll be left with a single loop, and you can again skip one stitch and repeat the previous step.

9. As you can see, this pattern isn't difficult. But, you need to be mindful of how tight your thread is. It shouldn't be too tight, or else the blanket won't be soft enough.

10. Keep doing the half-double crochet cross stitches along the second row.

11. But, how to finish a row? The row should close by doing a half-double crochet, chaining two, and rotating the work.

12. There are a couple of things to be mindful of when learning how to do this stitch.

13. You should take the time so that you won't skip stitches or use the same chain/gap twice.

14. Secondly, the more rows you crochet, the harder it might be to see through the work and know where your hook should go. For this reason, be extra careful and mindful of where you're inserting the hook.

15. Proceed with this new stitch until you've made all of your rows.

16. This stitch is a bit more complex, but it produces a thick, consistent, yet soft and snuggly throw or blanket that will be more functional than decorative.

17. The chunkier the yarn, the better will the blanket will look and feel. But, using extra chunky yarn will make it even more difficult to keep your stitches in check and will require extra time.

The amount of yarn you'll need will depend on the desired size of the blanked.

A baby blanket will require 900 grams, or 981 yds, with 66 chains and 54 rows. A small throw will need 1,400g of chunky yarn or 1526yds, and you'll need 92 chains with 60 rows.

Pattern #7:

The Simple Stitch Afghan

Requirements:

- **Yarn:** Size five.
- **Hook**: 12 mm.

One great thing about this pattern is that you will be using a single stitch throughout the entire blanket. This time you will use two different-colored balls of yarn for extra variety.

Instructions:

1. Chain 70 stitches by yarning over and pulling through.

2. Proceed with a chain-two and work into the third stitch from the beginning.

3. This means to count the first hole next to your hook as first, the next one as the second, and then insert the hook into the hole after it.

4. After you yarn over and pull through the third stitch, you'll have three loops on your hook.

5. To finish the stitch, yarn over and pull through all three loops. Proceed until the end of the row.

6. As you get close to the end of the row, chain two and turn the work.

7. Proceed using the same pattern, this time inserting the hook into the second hole instead of the third.

8. Once you get to the end of the row, you'll find that you're missing a stitch that would make the work even.

9. Here, you should simply hook into the stitch from the previous, bottom row that sticks out, yarn over, and pull through.

10. Now, your work will be even, you can chain tow, and turn it over to begin the next row. Proceed until you've made a desired number of rows!

11. Once you get to the end of the blanket, clip the yarn, yarn over, and pull through once more.

12. Tie the knot and weave the extra yarn in.

Pattern #8:

A Square-Patterned Blanket

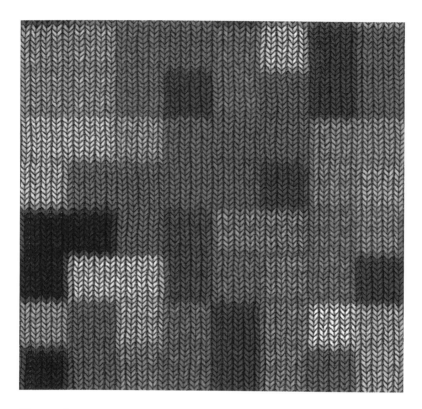

Requirements:

- **Yarn**: size 3 yarn, 2400m or 2624 yds
- **Hook**: H8 or a 9 mm hook.

Instructions:

1. For this blanket, start by chaining a foundation and then chain the base row until the desired size.

2. Yarn over into the third loop from the base chain and pull through.

3. You now have three loops. Yarn over and pull through all three loops.

4. Put one half-double crochet into each chain until the end of the row.

5. Chain one and turn the work over.

6. Put a half-double crochet into the first space, yarn over and pull through, and then yarn over and pull through all three loops.

7. Then, skip one space and work a half-double crochet into the next spot, yarn over and pull through, and then yarn over and pull through the remaining loops.

8. Repeat until the end of the row.

9. Once you reach the end of the row, insert the hook into the bottom change that's sticking out, yarn over and pull through, chain one, and turn the work over.

10. Work a half-double crochet into the next space, skip a space, and work a single crochet in the next space.

11. Repeat the half-double crochet after every single crochet until the end of the row.

This pattern will create a distinct square shape from your yarn and, if you combine multiple yarn colors, the texture of the work will stand out even more. Keep in mind that, unlike the previous pattern, this one is done with thin, fine yarn that might be a bit more difficult to work with. However, the blanket will have a fine, intricate texture that can work for baby blankets, king and queen-size afghans, and even shawls.

Pattern #9:

The Afghan Cluster Stitch

After finishing the previous blanket, you may have begun to understand the logic behind creating square and rectangle shapes. It's all about knowing when to skip a space, and what happens when you are combining single, double, and triple crochets. Does it extend or reduce chain lengths? You need to know these things to create the shapes you wish to make. For this project, you'll start making more round shapes which, in multi-color yarn, resemble having small circles attached. With that in mind, let's start crocheting a bit more complex stitches and shapes:

Requirements:

- **Yarn:** Size four.
- **Hook:** an L9 or a 5.5 mm.

Instructions:

1. As usual, start with a slipknot and a base chain.

2. Work the next row into the second chains, yarn over and pull through, and then proceed by skipping one stitch and then chaining one into the next.

3. Do a final double stitch into the final stitch of the row.

4. Chain four and turn the work around.

5. You'll now start making your clusters.

6. Yarn over into the first gap, pull through the first loops.

7. Yarn over again through the gap, pull up, yarn over, and pull through two loops.

8. Now, you have four loops on your hook.

9. Again, insert the hook into the gap, yarn over and pull the thread up, yarn over, and pull through.

10. Once more, yarn over and pull through two loops.

11. You now have a total of five loops on your hook.

12. Finally, yarn over and pull through all five loops.

13. Chain up to secure the cluster stitch.

14. Repeat throughout all of the chain spaces until the end of the row.

15. Once you reach the end, do a treble stitch to finish the row. Chain one and turn the work over.

16. Do a double crochet into the space between the clusters until the end of the row.

17. Finish the row with a double crochet into the last space.

18. Do a treble, chain four, and turn the work over.

19. For this row, continue by making cluster stitches as described.

20. Once you reach the end of the row, proceed with the next by doing a double crochet into spaces between clusters.

21. Finish the blanket with a row of double crochets so that the edges are even.

Pattern #10:

Tunisian Knit Stitch

Was making those clusters a bit overwhelming? While your blanket is probably beautiful, it's also likely that you're exhausted from doing all that intricate work. Now, you'll unwind a little bit with some Tunisian knit stitching, which might serve as a bit of crochet cardio here. Tunisian knit stitch is one of the most functional forms of crochet, it's repetitive and simple to do, and it's also great to practice speed, focus, and precision with crocheting. This stitch is easiest to practice with chunky yarn, but doing it with finer, thinner yarn will result in more consistent, fabric-like work. This is something to keep in mind in case you wish to make a more sleek-looking throw that doesn't have a lot of fluffiness and doesn't appear chunky or fluffy.

Requirements:

- **Yarn:** Size four.
- **Hook:** 6 mm.

I recommend two complementing colors, and of course, a medium yarn so that it's easier to work with.

Instructions:

Here are the steps for this pattern:

1. First, crochet your chain in the desired length.
2. Now, let's start with your first row.
3. Count the last loop from the base chain as your first stitch and simply turn the work over, inserting the hook into the closest stitch.
4. Yarn over, pull through. This time, don't finish the stitch by pulling through two loops. Instead, keep the loop on the hook, insert it into the next stitch, yarn over, and pull through until you reach the end of the row.
5. With this pattern, each of your rows will have a border stitch.
6. To make it, simply insert the hook into the last stitch, yarn over and pull the thread through,

and then yarn over and pull through only the last loop on the hook.

7. After that, yarn over and pull through two loops until you're left with a single loop.

8. To start the next row, simply insert the hook between the second two stitches, yarn over, pull the thread through, and repeat the process while keeping the loops on your hook.

9. Repeat the previous steps and yarn over and pull through two loops once you reach the end of the row.

10. If you wish to work with two different colors, you can do so by pulling in a second color as you're yarning over for the final stitch of a row.

11. To finish the last row, don't leave the loops on your hook. Instead, yarn over and pull through each of the loops, and your blanket will have a clean, even edge that resembles the chain base you started with.

Pattern #11:

The Basket Weave Stitch

Requirements:

- **Yarn:** Size five.
- **Hook:** 6 mm.

Instructions:

1. Start your chain and follow with a row of double crochet into the third chain from the hook.

2. Chain two, turn the work, and put your hook around the back of the bottom chain, and

proceed with double crochets in the next four chains.

3. Once you get to the fifth chain, you will reverse the process.

4. Yarn over and hook around the back of the stitch, yarn over and pull through, and do a double crochet.

5. Repeat for three more stitches. These four stitches will now appear as an independent.

6. Proceed with four more 'front' stitches, and then four 'back' stitches.

7. Once you get to the end of the row, yarn over and insert the hook into the stitch that's sticking out and do a half-double crochet.

8. Chain two and turn the work over.

9. Proceed to finish the row. You should now have finished a total of three rows.

10. The fourth row will start by doing 'back' stitches into the bottom 'front' stitches to create a contrast, while the 'back' stitches will be followed by the 'front' stitches in the new row.

11. Proceed with the same pattern for the fifth and sixth row, and switch again at the seventh.

12. Finish the work by doing a half-double crochet over the final row.

Pattern #12:

The Waffle Stitch

This pattern is great for smaller pieces like washcloths and baby blankets. If you wish for your crochet to be machine washable and functional, you should go for cotton yarn.

Requirements:

- **Yarn:** Size three.
- **Hook:** 4 mm.

Instructions:

1. Start with a chain of the desired size. Work a double crochet into the first chain of the base row.

2. Do another double crochet into the remaining stitches until the end of the row.

3. Start the second row by chaining one, turning the work over, and do a double crochet into the first noticeable gap.

4. To create the "waffle" effect, the next double crochet won't be done by going into the gap, but instead by inserting the hook behind a chain from the bottom row.

5. You need to yarn over, insert the needle behind the chain, have the hook appear on the other end, yarn over, and pull the hook through, or in this case, behind the chain.

6. Again, pull through two loops until you have a single loop.

7. The next two double crochet will again be through the top stitches and the third will be behind the chain of the bottom row.

8. This is the pattern that will create the waffle texture.

9. When you get to the last stitch, do a double crochet into the last stitch.

10. Chain one, turn the work over, and pay attention to which chains to push forward.

11. The following row will have an opposite direction, meaning that you'll work two double crochets behind the chains of the bottom row, and the third will be into the top stitch.

12. Proceed until the end of the row, work a double crochet into the stitch that's sticking out, chain two, and start the next row.

13. Work two double crochets into top chains and the third behind the bottom-row chain.

14. To finish the work, run a series of double crochets into each of the top stitches.

Pattern #13:

The Diamond Stitch Afghan

How about an Afghan that features wonderful, diamond-resembling texture? This Afghan is suitable for chunky yarn and particularly great if you intend on making an extra functional Afghan to serve its main purpose—keep you warm. If you are making baby blankets, this stitch is great because it can be used with cotton and hypoallergenic yarn. It is also great for washcloths and, if you use a decorative thread, it will make for an amazing tablecloth. So, how do you start with this Afghan?

Requirements:

- **Yarn:** Size two to four.
- **Hook**: 3.5-6mm.

Instructions:

1. Your first step will be to learn how to make a diamond stitch.

2. This stitch may look complex, but it's quite easy to learn.

3. Create the base chain and do single crochets into each stitch on the base.

4. Repeat for the second row.

5. For the third row, chain one, and do a front post double crochet into the second single crochet of the first row.

6. Single crochet into the next three stitches.

7. Proceed with a front post double crochet into the coordinating stitch in the first row.

8. Repeat for the fourth stitch in that row.

9. Proceed with a single crochet into the following three stitches in row three.

10. Repeat doing the two front posts followed by three single crochets until the end of the row.

11. Start the fourth row by chaining two, turning the work, adding a double crochet into the first

stitch, proceeding with double crochets into each stitch until the end of the row.

12. For the next row, chain one and turn the work.

13. Do a single crochet into the first stitch and the one after that, and do two front post double crochets together as already described.

14. This time, you will do the second by inserting the needle into the top corner of the two conjoined double crochets.

15. Do three more double crochets into the stitches of the row, and proceed to do the two front posts as already described.

16. Proceed until the end of the row.

17. For the next row, chain two and work a double crochet into the first stitch, and each stitch until the end of the row.

18. Chain one for the next row, and proceed doing two front posts behind each of the front post chains of the previous row.

19. Continue until you finish your work!

Now that you know how to do a diamond stitch, I suggest that you start making your first swatches. A lot can be done to visually enrich this pattern, from switching two or three colors for every other row, which will make it look like the colors are overlapping, to creating a block-like structure by switching yarn after each rectangular sequence. Furthermore, I recommend being extra mindful of your tension.

Making a fabric that's too tight might make it more difficult to do front and back post stitches, and the result may look awkward. If your yarn isn't loose enough, what's supposed to resemble diamonds might simply look like tiny flaws in your work. A yarn that's too tight might curl to the point where these distinct shapes no longer shine through, so make sure that your yarn is nice and loose!

Pattern#14:

The Textured Wave Stitch

This stitch stretches nicely, and it's also dense enough for a cozy Afghan. While it works well with all types of yarn, you're best off using medium-weight yarn. However, this stitch is highly convenient for a robust throw or thick, sturdy rug. With this in mind, feel free to use thicker yarns as well.

Requirements:

- **Yarn:** Size four.
- **Hook**: 5.5 mm.

Instructions:

Here's how to make an easy textured wave Afghan:

1. For the base row, chain a desired number of stitches, adding six at the end.

2. You can use standard stitch and chain guides for an Afghan of your desired size, or rely on a measuring tape to decide how many chains you need based on a swatch.

3. For the first row, slip stitch into the second stitch from the hook and the following four.

4. The next five stitches are done with half double crochets, and then alternating between the slip stitch and the half-double until the end of the row.

5. For the second row, chain one, slip stitch into the first five stitches, and proceed to do half double crochets into the next five.

6. Repeat until the end of the row.

7. Do the third and fourth row starting with five half-double stitches, and then the fifth by starting with slip stitches.

8. Repeat the pattern for rows two to five until you finish your blanket!

Who would say that this interesting texture can be achieved by simply varying two different sequences? As you can see, making this Afghan is as simple as it can get. Feel free to alter colors as you wish, but rest assured that your blanket will look amazing whichever color you choose.

Now, as you reach the end of this chapter, it's time to take your game to the next level. The next stitch that you're going to learn is beginner-friendly because it's repetitive, but it is only slightly more complex compared to other beginner stitches.

Pattern#15:

The Shell Stitch Afghan

As its name suggests, the shell stitch creates a nice, ornamental, shell-looking pattern for your Afghan. The fabric it produces will have a fun, elegant pattern, but it still won't have a lot of holes. Aside from Afghans and washcloths, it is also great for scarves and shawls. This stitch looks great when done using thread as well, and can be used to make beautiful, flowy skirts, dresses, and shawls. But, you're here to learn how to make a shell stitch Afghan. To start, I recommend making a fabric sample and then calculating the size and the amount of yarn that you used to determine how many chains, stitches, and yarn you will need for a full Afghan.

Requirements:

- **Yarn:** Size two to four.
- **Hook**: 2.5-5.5 mm.

Instructions:

Here are the steps for making a shell stitch Afghan:

1. To do this stitch, make a base chain that measures five chains for each shell plus one stitch.

2. Make sure to keep your yarn on the looser side so that the shells are easier to notice.

3. If the tension is too tight, they might appear too constricted and resemble popcorn or bean stitches instead.

4. Chain one to start the second row and do one single crochet into the stitch next to the hook.

5. Skip two and do five doubles into the next stitch. Skip two, and do a single crochet into the third stitch from the base.

6. This will form your first shell.

7. Repeat the pattern of skipping two, working five doubles into the third stitch, again skipping two, and doing a single crochet into the third, skipping two, and doing five doubles into the third.

8. You can crochet as many shell-shaped rows as you please!

9. That's it! Your shells will form as you go, and you're only left with completing as many rows as you like!

Upon finishing your shell stitch Afghan, you can either leave it with wavy edges or create a frame for even edges. If you decide to make a frame for your Afghan, you can do this easily by first connecting the tops of the shells with chaining. Once you have a flat edge across your blanket, you can proceed to add single crochets, double crochets, or any other simple stitch that you like around your Afghan. If you wish to increase the size, this is the easiest and fastest way to do it. Furthermore, you can add a contrasting color to your frame or use the same yarn that you used for the blanket if you wish for it to remain a single color.

Great job! You already know how to make 15 beginner Afghans! Now, it's time to take your skills further, to the intermediate level. Before you begin with your intermediate stitches and patterns, I recommend practicing crochet samples or swatches for the stitches and patterns shown in this chapter. That way, you'll not only polish your skills but also improve the speed of your work. The more your practice these basic, repetitive stitches, the better you automate the micro-movements needed for more complex work. Making granny squares and other motifs will be a lot easier if you don't have to fully concentrate on each single and double crochet, so take your time practicing. If you feel like you're ready, then hop on the intermediate wagon!

Chapter 4:

5 Intermediate Afghan Patterns

In this chapter, you'll learn how to make granny squares or blocks. Granny squares are among the most popular motifs for Afghans and even knowing the basic ones opens a whole new world of possibilities for you. While stitches and patterns used to make these squares vary, the sequences of the work are roughly similar. Typically, granny square Afghans are made in four distinct stages:

- **Center motifs.** The designs shown in this chapter will be simple and easy to make, but unlike the beginner ones, these will have more dimensions. More importantly, they will be done in rounds rather than rows. This means that you'll learn how to create angles, circles, floral shapes, and all other lines and contours using chains.

- **Square frames.** After finishing your center motifs, you're going to have to frame them to create an even square shape. This way, you will be able to join multiple, dozens, or even hundreds of squares into a single Afghan.

- **Square joining.** After learning how to complete granny squares, you need to learn how to join them to put the Afghan together. As you'll later learn, this can be done in several ways, from amateur-friendly to professional.

- **Blanket framing.** Lastly, after completing and joining all of your squares, you should also learn how to make decorative frames for them. Frames create clean, even edges, and prevent the blanket from folding or curling at the joints.

Are you ready? Let's start making intermediate Afghan patterns!

Pattern #1:

The Beginner Granny Square

Now that you have learned over a dozen different Afghan stitches, it's time to start making granny squares! As you learned, granny squares are somewhat of a staple design everyone thinks about when you mention Afghans, and not without a reason. Granny squares can be taken from traditional to modern, and from elegant to shabby chic with a snap of a finger. Learning how to crochet granny squares opens many doors in terms of how you express your style. The beginner granny square pattern is similar to patterns 13 and 14, and it's beginner-friendly because the square itself is done in a single, repetitive pattern. Still, it gives you plenty of space to switch color combinations for each square, and have as much or as little variety in your Afghan as you please.

One thing I noticed with people who are just learning how to make granny squares is that they get intimidated when they see multiple different crochet stitches and styles varied within the same design. Combined with a multitude of colors this looks great but, when you're the one who is supposed to make the design, it may appear a lot more difficult than it is. Remember, beginner or not, granny squares simply vary multiple similar stitches and patterns to create a unique design for each square.

Requirements:

- **Yarn:** Size four.
- **Hook**: 5.5 mm.

Instructions:

If you want to make an Afghan that looks like over ten different styles are used, don't worry. Chances are that only two or three different patterns are used and varied throughout the entire work. With that in mind, let's begin (Moore & Prain, 2019):

1. As always, start with a desired length base chain that you'll determine the length of.
2. Decide on the size and number of squares you wish to use for your blanket.

3. Create a staple stitch count for each block or rectangle. This will simplify the process in your mind and you'll feel more confident in your work.

4. Unlike typical crochet, the base chain for the granny square will be smaller, as you'll be crocheting around it.

5. This pattern will use a chain four for the base.

6. Once you get to the fourth chain and insert the hook into the last loop from the other side.

7. Yarn over and pull through. You will get a circle with a hole in the middle.

8. Pick up the thread yarn and hold it next to the reign to weave it in seamlessly as you crochet.

9. Chain three and do two more double crochets into the ring's hole and two more double crochets.

10. You will now have three double crochets sticking out from the ring.

11. Chain two and work three double crochets through the gap of the ring.

12. You'll notice that you've now created a corner.

13. Do another three double crochets in the same fashion, and you now need to connect the angle of the work.

14. You'll do this by chaining two, making three more double crochets, and then close the gap by

chaining one and finding the top loop in the opposite chain.

15. Hook into the top loop, yarn over and pull through, and then yarn over and pull through the two remaining loops.

16. Your first square is now finished, and you'll proceed to crochet around it in the same fashion.

17. Chain three, turn the work, and chain two double crochets into the gap inside the corner of the work.

18. Yarn over and insert the hook into the gap of the next corner, adding three double crochets into it as well.

19. Chain two and repeat for the next corner.

20. Chain two, turn the work, and proceed working three double crochets into each corner.

21. Finally, connect the corners by doing a chain one into the top loop of the opposite chain.

22. Chain three, turn the work over, add two more double crochets into the corner.

23. Proceed by adding three double crochets into each gap you encounter.

24. Once you're finished with your square, which will, in this case, be when you reach the closing gap for the third row, you can either tie a knot and snip off the thread, weave the thread in, or make tassels if you please.

Now that you know how to make a basic granny square, you can use it in several ways to create Afghans. You crochet around your base square until you reach the desired size or you can make multiple different squares and sew them together. You can also proceed to crochet one-piece Afghans from granny squares, which you'll learn in the next pattern.

Pattern #2:

Border-And-Join Granny Square Afghan

Now, let's start making a bit more complex granny-square pattern. This pattern doesn't only join multiple granny squares together, but it also uses different colors for the square borders. For the sake of this tutorial, let's choose a pink and white color. Your first square will have a white interior and will be framed by pink wool crochet.

Requirements:

- **Yarn:** Size four.
- **Hook**: 5.5 mm.

Instructions:

Here's how to do it:

1. Chain five loops, and then make a ring as per the previous instruction.

2. Proceed to build your granny square by chaining three, doing two double crochets, and then doing three more sets or clusters of double crochets, joining the corners as per the previous instructions until your block is finished.

3. To start making a contrasting border, in this case, a pink border over your white square, pull the hook through one of the gaps along the square's other edges, pull up a loop, and chain three.

4. You will now begin crocheting a border.

5. If you're using chunky yarn, it won't matter much if you choose one of the gaps on the flat sides of the block.

6. But, if you're working with a thinner, finer yarn, I'd recommend starting from the corners, since they already break that visual balance of the piece, and one extra peaking stitch won't show as much.

7. After you've chained three, crochet two more double crochets into the same gap.

8. Proceed by adding three double crochets into each of the gaps.

9. Once the border is finished, snip off the yarn, and weave in the ends.

10. Now, you can begin joining your squares. Remember, when joining dozens of squares into a blanket, it's always better to work along the shorter edges of the work.

11. To start joining squares, lay them one on top of the other with their back sides touching so that the one right side faces you, and the other faces your table or surface.

12. Insert your hook through the corner caps of both squares, pull the yarn through, tie it, yarn over, and chain one.

13. Now, you'll be crocheting over the edge of the squares you wish to join.

14. Make sure to insert the hook into the same spots or gaps of both squares, and yarn over and pull through twice.

15. Proceed by doing a double crochet into the top of each double crochet frame chain by making sure to insert the hook through both squares.

16. Every time you reach a gap in the frame, do a single crochet. Finish the crochet once you reach the end of the edge.

That's it! You've now joined your first two squares. You can use this simple method to make a blanket out of as many different granny squares as you like! Now that you know how to do all this, let's learn one different granny square pattern, plus one more joining method, shall we?

Pattern #3:

The Simple Granny Rectangle Afghan

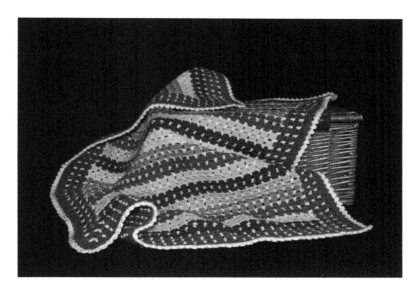

Now that you know how to make a bit more complex stitches, let's make your first geometric Afghan. I recommend that you stay focused on the pattern and instructions, because, for a beginner, looking at a finished rectangle Afghan may be intimidating. The work may seem too complex and difficult, while it isn't. This stitching, however, demands your full focus. Unlike simpler stitches like the fishbone or Tunisian can be done while you're relaxing and watching TV, rectangle patterns require attention, counting stitches, and being mindful of where to put your hook. With that in mind, you can begin:

Requirements:

- **Yarn:** Size four.
- **Hook**: 5.5 mm.

Instructions:

1. Start with a usual base chain.

2. Start the first one and hook into the fourth chain.

3. Double crochet and do another double crochet into that same stitch.

4. Chain one, skip two chains, and add three double crochets into that chain.

5. Skip two more chains and add two double crochets. Repeat until the end of the row.

6. Chain two, turn the corner, and do three double crochets into the first top of the bottom rectangle.

7. Continue the same pattern of hooking three double crochets into the top chain of each bottom rectangle.

8. Continue until the end of the row.

9. Once you start the third row, do three slip stitches into the top chain.

10. This chain will be the bottom of a rectangle from the previous row.

11. Start the first rectangle of your third row by hooking into the chain above the gap between the rectangles from the bottom row.

12. Do three double crochets and make rectangles above the gap between bottom rectangles.

13. Finish the row, chain two, turn the work over, and start again by using the same pattern starting from step four.

14. Proceed until you achieve the desired size of the Afghan, and then finish the work using your favorite method.

15. You can either simply snip the excess yarn and tie a knot (less preferred among professionals), weave the thread in, crochet around the Afghan to create a nice frame or add tassels.

Voila! You now have your first rectangle Afghan, and it was a lot easier to make than you thought, wasn't it? Now, let's learn another variation of the granny rectangle that uses a similar pattern, but the work comes out a little bit smaller and thicker.

Pattern #4:
Granny Rectangle Version 2.0

This pattern is a little bit smaller compared to the previous one. It is done using a smaller hook, and instead of working into the chains of the previous row, you will crochet around the chains so that the rectangles are more tightly connected:

Requirements:

- **Yarn:** Size four.
- **Hook:** 5.5 mm.

Instructions:

1. After making your first chain, chain three and insert the hook into the bottom of the first chain, and do a double crochet.

2. Yarn over and insert the hook into the next chain.

3. Do three double crochets, skip two chains, and work three double crochets into each third chain.

4. Close the row by adding two double crochets to the final chain by chaining three, inserting the hook into the last remaining chain, and then doing the two double crochets.

5. Chain three and proceed by adding three double crochets into each of the little gaps above the top of the rectangles.

6. Once you get to the opposite side, chain four and do another two clusters of three double crochets into the corner.

7. This will produce an angle, and you may proceed until the end of the row.

8. Once you get to the next corner, chain one and do three double crochets into the corner.

9. Chain three and do three more double crochets into the next flat chain.

10. Proceed crocheting the pattern until the end of the row.

11. Once you get to the end of the row, you will now do two double crochets into the corner, insert the hook into the third chain of the other side to connect the sides into a new cluster, chain three, and do two more double crochets into the bottom chain.

12. Work around the edges and finish the work by inserting the hook into a stitch from the connecting rectangle.

13. You may proceed to finish the Afghan as you please!

Pattern #5:

The Griddle Crochet Afghan

This stitch creates a rectangle effect and I like it because you can achieve a similar, granny-square-like pattern while doing a bit simpler crochet. At the same time, this pattern can combine multiple colors easily, without having to crochet individual squares and then stitch them together. I recommend choosing a very light, medium, and dark shade of the same color for a subtle, gradiating effect. However, this pattern can also be done with two different hooks—one for the chain and one for the blanket. If you use a smaller hook for the base, like a size H or I, the base will have a bit more distinct shape. But, you can still work with a single hook, either an I or an H, and your work will turn out beautiful. You'll need two skeins of the middle shade, and one of each—the darkest and lightest shade.

Requirements:

- **Yarn:** Size four.
- **Hook**: 6 mm.

Instructions:

Here's how to do this stitch:

1. Start your base chain using one size smaller hook, and then switch to a bigger hook for your work.

2. Do a single crochet into the first chain and follow up with a double crochet.

3. Switch colors every 10 stitches, which will create a square effect as you go along.

4. Alternate the colors as you go along.

5. The entire Afghan is done by working a single crochet into a chain, then doing a double crochet into the next stitch, and then again a single crochet.

6. Here, the size of your blocks will depend on how many stitches you crochet with a single color.

7. Keep in mind to crochet a color, you alternate colors into the work by pulling its thread into the base each time you hook into the chain.

8. That way, when you finish a series of stitches with a desired color, you can alternate simply.

While this pattern isn't difficult, make sure to alternate colors after each 10 by 10-stitch block of the same color. Another tip is to make sure to choose extra soft yarn and avoid adding too much tension to your work. If the work is too tight, it will resemble a rug. On that note, you can use this stitch to make a rug. All you need to do is choose a thicker yarn that's more suited to the purpose and keep the work tense and firm.

Great job! you're almost ready to start making some of the most demanding and challenging afghan patterns! This chapter gave you the basics for making larger motifs that are typical for robust, luxury Afghans. In the next chapter, you'll learn how to apply this knowledge to make and combine various motifs into an advanced design. So, what are you waiting for? Let's start doing advanced Afghan crochet!

Chapter 5:

5 Advanced Afghan Patterns

What makes an Afghan pattern advanced? If you look at a pattern carefully, even the one that seems the hardest to do, you'll notice that it can be broken down into sequences of alternating stitches and patterns. Still, some motifs and patterns need to be worked in multiple stages and require a lot more than just printing a pattern and choosing. The patterns given in this chapter will require you to first read through the instructions, practice, and make swatches, and then plan the size of your project and necessary materials accordingly.

Furthermore, these patterns will require a good grip of complex stitches, like the cross-stitch, the front and back post double crochets, and others. Keep in mind that understanding how these stitches are done and successfully making a project out of them isn't the same. You'll need practice for the stitches to start coming out naturally, meaning that you need to form the muscle memory to make these complex stitches in a relaxed, spontaneous manner. As you read through the following patterns, take your time to practice along the way and make your swatches. With that in mind, here are some of the most intricate, yet beautiful, advanced crochet patterns to try out:

Pattern #1:

The Star-Crossed Afghan

You can make this triangular, star-like motif using gradating complementary colors that range either from the lightest in the center to the darkest for exterior edges, or vice versa. My recommendation is to choose the first option since it will make the wonderful star motif stand out. Your pattern will consist of two motifs, which you can join using your preferred stitching—it can be either single or double crochet depending on the size or the style you prefer.

For this Afghan, you'll need a 5.5 mm hook, or the size L/9. You'll be crocheting around five stitches for an inch of the fabric. As always, you can alter the yarn and the hook size, but here, I'll recommend the beginner-friendly size four yarn. As always, I recommend doing swatches of both motifs beforehand to measure your gauge.

Requirements:

- **Yarn:** Size four worsted yarn, approx. 58 oz (mixed colors/monochrome) for approx 53x75"
- **Hook:** L-9 or 5mm

Instructions:

My sizes average four by six inches for the motif, while the finished size averages 53-55 by 75-78 inches. Yours doesn't have to fully match, given that you might be using different yarn or tension. For this size, I used a total of 58 ounces of different-colored yarn. Here are the steps:

1. Chain four and make a ring with a slip stitch to start your **first motif**.
   a. For the first round, chain one, and then add this pattern twice into the loop: single, half-double, triple crochet, chain three, triple, double, and the half-double crochet.
   b. Close the round with a slip stitch.
   c. For the second round, chain five, and add a double, a single, a chain one.

d. Add a double crochet in the following three stitches.

e. Next, you will add the following stitches into the space of the third chain: three double crochets, four-chain, three double crochets.

f. Finish the pattern with double crochets into the next three stitches, and repeat until you finish the round.

g. For the third round, chain three, and these stitches to the chain-two space: double, three-chain, double crochet.

h. Double-crochet into the next two stitches, chain one, skip one, and add a double crochet to the next chain.

i. Again, chain and then skip one, and add the following stitches to space after that: three doubles, a five-chain, three doubles. Chain and skip one, and work double crochets into the next three stitches.

j. Work two more double crochets into the next two chains, and repeat the previous step. Add a double crochet to the last chain, close off.

2. Now, it's time to start making the **second motif.**

a. Work the first two rounds as per the previous instruction, and start round three by chaining three.

b. For the third round, add a double crochet into the space of the second chain, chain one, and start slip stitching to the first motif's chain three space.

c. Chain one and work a double crochet into the second motif's second chain space, and then double crochet into the next two stitches.

d. Add a single crochet to the next chain space, and skip one double crochet, adding another into the next three double crochet chains.

e. Join the stitches and work three doubles into the chain space, and then chain two and work a single crochet into the next chain space of the first star motif.

f. Chain two, work three double crochets into the space of the four-chain on the motif in progress and complete by closing off the round so that only one side of the motif is joined.

g. You will be joining these motifs as you go, so I recommend doing single crochets into the singles of the previous joint when putting all of the motifs together.

h. This will, most likely, be the spots where multiple stitches from different parts are joined together.

3. Now, it's time to make the **frame motif.**

a. This motif starts with a four-chain closed into a ring, and then followed by chain one.

b. Turn single, half-double, double, triple crochets, and then chain three.

c. Go in reverse, do a triple, double, half-double, and single crochet.

d. The second round begins with a three-chain and double crochets into the first four stitches from your hook.

e. The next pattern goes into the chain space: three double crochets, four-chain, and three double crochets.

f. Then, you are to add double crochets into the next three stitches and two doubles into the last chain.

g. For the third round, turn the work and start joining to your complete motif by chaining three and doing a single crochet into that motif.

h. Again, chain one, work three doubles into the first three double crochets of the previous round, join to the previous motif, double-crochet into the next three stitches, join again and repeat three doubles into the chain space.

i. Then, chain two and work single crochets into the joint.

j. Then, chain two and add three doubles into the previous chain space, join, and double crochet into the next three stitches, again join and double-crochet into the next two double-crochet chains.

k. Now, do one double crochet into the top of the three-chain, chain one, and do a single crochet into the chain space of the joining motif.

l. Chain three and close the round off with a slip stitch.

4. Once you're done making and joining your motifs, it's time to work around the **edges** of your Afghan.

a. Attach the completed work with the right side facing you using any stitch you like.

b. Proceed with single stitching evenly around the work, making sure to keep the Afghan flat by increasing tension at outer points and decreasing it towards the inner points.

c. For the second round, chain three and work a round of double crochets into the chains of the work, while being mindful of the tension.

d. Finally, once you're finished, you can chain three and close off the round, fasten off, and choose the right method to weave the ends in.

Pattern #2:

The "Mandala" Effect Afghan

Do you enjoy coloring mandalas? If so, you're probably familiar with the intricacy of their fine shapes, and you're likely wondering how to possibly make similar Afghans. Luckily, you'll now get to work on one of those shapes, and even better, make a complete, luxury Afghan out of them. How? By following these simple steps:

For a single-size Afghan, you'll need between 50 and 70 balls of yarn, while the double size will require between 70 and 80 balls of yarn. I recommend working with a size seven hook. Each of the motifs average six inches in diameter, meaning that you'll need around 160 motifs for a 75x108" single. For a double, count on making 208 motifs for a 90x108" Afghan.

Requirements:

- **Yarn:** Approx. 70-80 balls of size three yarn
- **Hook:** 7 (4.5mm)-L/9 (5mm)

Instructions:

Your work will consist of two distinct motifs, a filler motif, and the edging, meaning that you'll do the entire work in four stages:

1. For the **first motif**, chain and ring six in the center.

    a. After joining with the slip stitch, start the first round by chaining four, and then adding 15 triple crochets in the center.

    b. After joining with the first chain four that you made, begin the second round.

    c. For round two, chain seven and repeat the following steps: do triple crochets into the next triple crochet chain from round two, and chain three.

    d. Proceed with triple crochets until you reach the end of the round, join with the first chain on the fourth stitch, and again chain four for the third round.

e. For the third round, chain four to start a pattern, which you'll repeat until the end: make a popcorn stitch in the first space, one triple crochet, and a popcorn stitch in that same space.

f. Do another triple crochet into the next triple chain, chain three afterward, and make another triple in the next triple crochet chain.

g. Once you close off the round, chain four and begin the fourth round.

h. For the fourth round, make a popcorn stitch using the same place where you put your slip stitch and begin a pattern to repeat until the end of the round: triple crochet into the popcorn stitch from the previous round, and then a popcorn stitch into the top chain of the triple crochet from the previous round.

i. As you can see, you are zigzagging the same pattern from round three until you finally close off.

j. For the fifth round, slip-stitch into the first popcorn stitch from the previous round and chain four. Since you already had two rounds of popcorn stitches expanding outwards, you'll now start reducing the pattern and bring it inwards.

k. Chain four and begin repeating this sequence: make a popcorn stitch in the triple crochet, and then make a triple crochet into the popcorn stitch from the previous round. Repeat twice and skip the next chain. Make five triple crochets into the chain space. This is to be repeated until you close off the round.

l. For round six, slip-stitch into the popcorn stitch and chain four. Do a triple crochet into the triple from the previous round and into the top chain of the popcorn stitch from the previous round.

m. Create a cluster by treating over and keeping the loops, so that you can pull through all of the loops and create a cluster.

n. Next, chain five and skip a triple and a space, adding two triples to the next triple chain, and then a triple to the next three stitches. Add two triples into the next chain, and then chain five.

o. Skip the chain space and make a triple crochet, followed by three stitches while you hold the remaining loop of each triple on your hook.

p. Make another cluster by pulling through all of the loops. Repeat the sequence from chain five onwards, and close off.

q. To begin round seven, chain eleven stitches, skip a space and a triple, and then work a triple crochet into the next five triple chains.

r. Each time you make a triple crochet, hold a loop so that you can pull through all of them to make a cluster.

s. Chain eleven on top of the next cluster and repeat the sequence. Once you finish the round, your motif will be done.

t. You can remove the excess thread and continue to make as many motifs as you'd like.

2. For the **second motif,** do the first six rounds as for the first motif.

a. Once you get to the seventh round, chain eleven, skip a space and a triple from the previous round, and add triples to the tops of the triple chains from the previous round.

b. Make sure to hold onto the loops so that you can pull through and make clusters.

c. Once you've made your clusters, chain five, and slip-stitch into the same loop on your first motif to connect them.

d. Chain five and slip-stitch into the next cluster of the current work.

e. Chain five and slip-stitch into the following 11 lops on your pattern. To complete the second motif, chain five and slip-stitch into the second motif.

f.   Chain five and slip-stitch into the next chain of the first work, and then again chain five, skip a space and a triple crochet, and finish off with a cluster from five triples on your ongoing motif.

g.   Finish the round and the work. After this, you can make the rest of the second motifs.

h.   Make sure that all of your motifs are joined, except for two eleven-chain loops, which should remain free.

3. Now, it's time to start making your **fill-in motifs**. These motifs consist of three rounds. For the first round, make a ring from eight chains.

a.   Then, make a triple crochet into the last chain twice, chain four, and slip-stitch into the fourth loop from that chain.

b.   To start a second round, chain four and make one popcorn stitch, followed by the triple crochet, and then another popcorn stitch.

c.   Once you get to the triple chain from the previous round, make one more triple, a six-chain, and another triple.

d.   Repeat the round sequence until you reach the end of the row and join the six-chain to the four-chain of the first motif.

e. Next, start the third round by chaining four and adding a triple crochet into each of the four slip-stitches to come, while holding onto the last loop from each triple to make a cluster.

f. Chain five and slip stitch into the free loop of the 11-chain of the first motif. Now, you will start a sequence to repeat until the end of the round—chain five and slip-stitch into the six-chain loop of the filler, again chain five, and do a slip-stitch into the large motif's 11-chain.

g. Chain five and add a triple crochet into the following five slipstitches as you hold onto the loops to make a cluster. After making a cluster, again, chain five, and slip-stitch into the largest chain, after which you'll repeat the sequence around until you reach the end of the round.

h. To finalize the filler, join the last five-chain using a slip-stitch to the top of the first cluster.

i. You can now finish the filler piece and proceed to make more.

4. Once all of your motifs and fillers are done and connected, you can start **edging** the work.

a. To do this, hook a thread into any joint between the motifs and work around using the following pattern—add seven slip stitches into each new motif's first loop.

b. For its following six loops, add one single, a half double, five doubles, four triples, five doubles, a half double, and a single crochet.

c. Proceed with making seven slip stitches into the loop before the next joint, and continue the pattern from the top.

Great job! If you persisted with making this pattern that means that you not only have an admirable skill set, but also plenty of patience and focus! Now that your Afghan is complete, you can throw it over a contrasting color to emphasize the lace effect that it has. The type and the color of the thread and the background are completely up to you!

Pattern #3:
Circular/"Sunshine" Granny Square Afghan

Although it's different from the basic granny square, the circular granny square actually consists of round crochet that's framed using the square pattern. With this in mind, let's begin crocheting:

Requirements

- **Yarn:** Size four, 50 yds./square
- **Hook:** L/9 or 5.5mm

Instructions:

1. Chain five for the center. If you want a bigger gap, you can use more stitches, while reducing the number of stitches on your chain will also reduce the gap.

2. The minimum number of base chains needed is three, in which case the center gap will be almost invisible.

3. Once you join the chain into a ring, chain three, and then add fifteen more double crochets.

4. Once you reach the edge or the first three-chain, hook into the top loop, pull the yarn through, and then insert the hook into one of the closest chains on the other side and pull the yarn through.

5. Tighten the circle to join the chains and weave in the remaining thread.

6. Now, pull a thread of yarn of different color through one of the stitches on the outer chain, pull it through, and chain seven more loops through that same gap.

7. Once you've counted seven chains, yarn over, and pull through all of the loops.

8. Yarn over, hook into the next chain space, and repeat the previous step.

9. Repeat along all of the chain spaces until you reach the end of the circle.

10. Slip stitch to close the round.

11. Pick up a yarn of a different color, and repeat steps 3-4 by adding cluster stitches into each of the border gaps or chain spaces.

12. For more variety, you can do four double crochets and then chain one once they're all joined to secure the cluster.

13. Circle along the base using your selected cluster stitch.

14. Once you finish your last cluster in the round, join the ends using the same method as in step two.

15. The border will be your final round.

16. Begin by adding a thread, chaining four, and doing three double crochets to create a corner.

17. Chain three and proceed to work double crochets into each of the chain spaces. Three-chains serve to form a corner, so don't use them between the double crochet clusters.

18. In the middle of the first sides, do three half-double crochet clusters.

19. Unlike the usual steps, if you wish to join the blocks to your crochet, you should add one more chain to the cluster through the corner of the square you wish to attach the work to.

20. Proceed with triple crochets for the corner and attach by hooking into a space between double crochets of a blanket with a slip stitch.

21. Proceed to frame the square with double crochets, but join each third chain of the cluster to its twin on the blanket using a slip stitch.

22. Once you get to the second corner, attach the corner of the frame you're making, now with a triple crochet, to the corner of the block next to the one you previously attached to.

23. Proceed to finish the frame as usual.

24. Remember the pattern for the corners! Corners are made using triple crochet clusters and then chaining three to begin another triple crochet cluster stitch. The remaining cluster stitches of your frame will be double crochet.

Wow, you've come so far! You already know how to make a large, beautiful granny square blanket! You can choose any color combination you like. Contrasting color will be fun to look at, while gradating colors will have a more elegant effect. Let's do one more granny square Afghan, shall we?

Pattern #4:

The Solid Granny Square Afghan

The solid square has a bit more neutral look. If you're not a fan of ornamental crochet and prefer something more simple, this style will be your best choice. Also, be mindful of the fact that the pattern has a reversible front and back, which is so you don't need to worry when joining squares together.

Requirements

- **Yarn:** Size four, 50 yds./square
- **Hook:** L/9 or 5.5mm

Instructions:

Here's how to make this nice-looking granny square:

1. Chain four and slip stitch into the first chain to create a loop. Chain two and do two more double crochets into the loop.

2. To make a corner, chain two and do two more double crochets into the loop. Do two more double crochets, chain two to make another corner, and close up with a slip stitch.

3. You now have a small square. To start the second round, chain two, and work two more double crochets into the corner gap.

4. Follow by doing double crochets into each of the stitches along the edge of the first round.

5. Add two double crochets into the corner gap, chain two, and proceed by adding one double crochet into each stitch until you reach the corner, where you'll add two double crochets.

6. Proceed until you close the round.

7. Chaining two before doing the double crochets for each corner will create the corner gap, so don't forget to do it!

8. Repeat steps 1-3 to crochet as many rounds as you like. You can make a bunch of blocks and join them together into a blanket, or proceed by adding rounds until you reach the desired blanket size.

There's a lot that you can do with this simple design to make it more fun and unique. You can change round colors and, of course, the order of colors for each individual square. This is a very tight pattern to begin with, so be extra mindful of tension and yarn when working. If you want a soft, cozy blanket, you should go for softer, chunkier yarn. However, if you want something thicker, like a rug, you can use thicker yarn for your work to be sturdy and straight. This pattern is also great for washcloths, given that you remember to use only machine washable cotton yarn. Finally, you can use this amazing pattern to make a tablecloth. In this case, go for thin, silky yarn, fresh-looking cotton yarn, or any other that will handle machine washing and daily use.

Pattern #5:

The Ornamental Afghan Square

Now that you learned how to make several types of Afghan squares, let's start using more decorative stitching for more lustrous, intricate works. The remaining pattern for our beginner section will be a little bit more complex, but combining them into a single afghan will be worth the effort.

Requirements

- **Yarn:** Size two-three, approx. 40-50 yds/square

- **Hook:** 4.5mm

Instructions:

For this square, you should use sleek, soft yarn with a 4.5 mm hook. Here are the steps:

1. Chain four and make a **ring**. Then, chain four, and proceed to do double crochets until you've made a total of 12.

   a. Once that's done, close the circle using a slip stitch.

   b. Proceed by chaining three and adding two or two double crochets into each gap between the chains of the circle, chaining two between each cluster.

   c. Once you're done with the round, chain two, and connect the sides with a slip stitch.

2. Start **round three** and do a double crochet into the first loop or gap between chain clusters.

   a. Chain seven, and proceed to do double crochets into gaps, followed by chaining two, chaining three-chains, and then a seven-stitch chain.

   b. You've now created a square, and you can slip stitch once you get to the end of the round.

3. Start the **fourth round** by doing a double crochet into the corner gap, chaining three, and

doing five more double crochets into the same gap.

a. Chain three and add another cluster to the corner. Do a double crochet into the next three-chain, chain four, and double crochet into the next space, and the third one.

b. Again, for the corner, do two clusters of five double crochets into the space where you chained seven stitches, chain three, and repeat for the remaining two sides.

c. Close the round with a slip stitch.

4. Start **round five** and pull the yarn through the first gap in the chain.

a. Repeat, chain one, and do double crochets into the next three stitches.

b. Do two double crochets into the space below the three-chain, chain three again to make a corner, chain four double crochets, chain four, and do a double crochet into the next space.

c. Repeat until you close the round.

5. To start **round six,** do four double crochets into the chain stitches, two double crochets into the corner gap, chain three, two more double crochets, and then again four double crochets.

a. Chain four, do two double crochets into the gap, chain four, and repeat for two more gaps.

b. Chain three and repeat the steps for the corner.

c. Close the round with a slip stitch once you get to the end.

6. Start **round eight** by doing double crochets into the next five stitches.

   a. Do two more doubles into the corner gap, chain three, two more doubles, and proceed from the beginning of the step until you close the round.

   b. Once you close the round, do two double crochets into the corner space, chain one, do two more double crochets, and then crochet doubles into each of the chain stitches.

   c. Once you get to the gaps, do two double crochets into chain spaces. Proceed for two more rows and you're done!

7. **Frame** your square by doing a double crochet into each of the chain stitches.

8. Proceed by making as many squares as you wish and joining them into an Afghan, a throw, or even a tablecloth if you wish by using your favorite method.

If you crochet squares one into the other, your fabric will be truly resilient and persistent. You won't have to pay that much attention to not pull on it, and it will be easier to use and wash. But, if you're making a baby blanket or a throw, which otherwise don't suffer as much usage or stress, you can sew in individual squares and go the easier route.

Additionally, remember to use cotton thread if you want your piece to be light, more decorative, and machine-washable. If you're making a soft, cozy throw, blanket, or shawl, you should go with either natural or acrylic wool.

Can you believe that you now know how to make no less than 25 different Afghans? Isn't that amazing? Hopefully, you now understand the logic behind making lustrous, intricate Afghans. Let's sum up common elements and phases of making an advanced Afghan:

- **The main motif.** The largest motif of the design is also known as the first or the main motif. It may repeat across the Afghan, or it can be distributed symmetrically across its surface. In some cases, only one of these complex motifs is used in a single Afghan. Usually, this stage is most difficult to do, since you don't yet have a sense of how big your work will turn out.

- **The second motif.** The alternate motif in a design is usually somewhat smaller than the main motif and made using similar patterns. As you might have noticed in the designs given in this chapter, some of the secondary motifs are made solely by following instructions for the first couple of rounds for the main motif.

- **The filler motif.** Of course, the Afghan's surface requires multiple smaller motifs to be filled in fully. These motifs are typically easiest to crochet, but more work is needed to join them to the rest of the work.

- **The joining stitches.** Finally, how you join your stitches can affect both the look and the size of your Afghan. Most advanced Afghans are joined as the motifs are being made, which requires extra counting and caution.

Conclusion

Great job! You now know how to make 25 amazing Afghan patterns, from beginner to expert! Wasn't this a fun ride? At the beginning of the book, you first learned that the Afghans came to the western countries from their country of origin, where the staple technique was used for fast, decorative, functional, and easy crochet.

You learned the main reasons why Afghan crochet became so popular so quickly. The techniques were simple to learn, the covers, blankets, and shawls were beautiful and functional, and more importantly, women were able to re-use some of their old yarn to make new items. You also learned how to crochet the beginner-friendly stitches that were known to be most suited for beginners.

As you learned, the Afghan crochet's amazing functionality also lies in the fact that you can use simple, repetitive, or alternate stitching to make anything from a washcloth to a king-size Afghan. But, as you learned, it's not all as easy as we'd like. Although simple and convenient, Afghan crochet requires you to know which stitches work well with which yarn, which hooks to use, and of course, to do careful math when modifying patterns and altering sizes. You also learned some of the most beautiful patterns out there still require you to fully focus and crochet patiently to avoid mistakes.

In this book, you also learned that the best way to learn new stitches is to make swatches or samples, and gradually learn and form muscle memory. You learned that, regardless of how complex certain patterns appear to be, they become easy once you reduce them to repetitive or alternating sequences of stitches. As you learned, even the most complex motifs can be broken down into rounds, and rounds can be further sequenced into a series of chains, single, double, and triple crochets. The more you learn and practice, the better you'll be able to recognize this simple combination of plain stitches in even the most complex-looking motifs.

In this book, you also learned that the best way to control the size of your work is to first make swatches and then use a measuring tape for the exact right size of your work. Of course, different patterns entail different counts of base chains and rows to achieve the desired size, and, as you learned, you are best off learning through your work than trusting the patterns and instructions too much.

After the beginner recommendations, you learned to make 15 beginner Afghans using simple, repetitive, or alternating stitches. Similar principles apply here as well, with chains, double, single, half-double, and triple crochets being used to form different shapes and textures. With this in mind, you can begin making your Afghans and, of course, experimenting with stitches to give your work a unique touch.

When you began learning about intermediate Afghan patterns, you learned how to make various granny squares, and at the same time, learn how to make somewhat complex motifs. The advantage of the motifs given in this book is that they are quite expressive and fun-looking. They give an impression of complex, intricate work when in reality, all you needed to do to make these squares was to repeat similar patterns across several rounds. You also learned multiple techniques to join motifs into a single Afghan and even how to crochet join motifs as you go!

Once you learned the beginner and intermediate techniques, the time came for you to learn how to make advanced, professional-level motifs and afghans. Here, you learned that to build truly ornamental, unique-looking afghans, one must break them down into the main and filler motifs, and of course, decide on the right stitching to frame your work. As you learned here as well, the motifs aren't very difficult to do. Once you figure out the order in which certain sequences repeat, everything becomes a lot easier. It appears that the most difficult technique to work with is crochet and join motifs as you go.

With this technique, you have to pay attention to when to attach one motif to another while still developing the new motif. But, with a little bit of persistence and experience, it will be easy for you to master this technique as well.

Finally, you learned some of the best ways to make unique Afghan crochet. If you're not keen on experimenting with stitches to create your own patterns, you can always make a unique blanket by simply alternating rows of different single stitches. Neat, right? Paired with some of the more complex stitches, like bean or shell, the filler rows of single stitches will give the work that staple functionality and thickness that you might be looking for.

Now that you're reaching the end of this book, I want to leave you with some useful recommendations and tips. First things first, the crochet skills are always a matter of practice. Even the most experienced crocheters remain humble and emphasize how important it is to try out new stitches and yarns regularly to maintain your crochet shape and muscle memory. If at this time, doing crochet still feels challenging, it is possible that you simply haven't yet practiced enough. Practice helps you automate many of the soft motor operations needed to complete the intricate stitches. Experienced crocheters do single and double crochets in a blink of an eye, simply because the movements become their second nature. They can do them accurately without having to put in as much as a thought.

While this might seem difficult to achieve, it is anything but. It's all a matter of how many thousand times are you ready to try out crochet and allow your mind and fingers to learn how to work together. If you're still struggling with beginner stitches-don't worry! There's a certain method to how we learn how to do new things and, for that learning to occur, practice is pivotal! Remember to always read the patterns, notice how many rounds are in the motif, and which particular stitches in those rounds are to be repeated. Create swatches based on these guidelines and you'll soon be able to tackle even the hardest patterns with true confidence and enthusiasm!

Exclusive 5-day bonus course just for you!

We will be sharing top crafting mistakes to avoid, how to save money on supplies and extra craft patterns!

Simply let us know where to send the course e-mails to via this link below.

https://bit.ly/nancy-gordon

For any general feedback & enquiries, you can reach us at bookgrowthpublishing@mail.com

References

Casey, C. (2013). *All About Crochet-A Beginner's Guide*. Lulu Press, Inc.

Goldberg, R. O. (1987). T*he New Crochet dictionary: Crochet Methods, Tools, Yarns, Symbols, Patterns, Motifs and Patchwork, Filet and Afghan Crochet, and More*. Crown Trade Paperbacks.

Moore, M., & Prain, L. (2019). *Yarn bombing: The art of crochet and knit graffiti*. Arsenal Pulp Press.

Made in the USA
Columbia, SC
17 December 2023

28792631R00088